P9-BIG-510

OF MARIN LIBRARY

FIELD CALIFORNIA

Vaughan Williams

VAUGHAN WILLIAMS

by

MICHAEL HURD

ML
410
V3H9
1970

THOMAS Y. CROWELL COMPANY

New York

Copyright © 1970 by Michael Hurd

All rights reserved. Except for use in a review, the reproduction or utilization of this work in any form or by any electronic, mechanical, or other means, now known or hereafter invented, including photocopying and recording, and in any information storage and retrieval system is forbidden without the written permission of the publisher.

Printed in Great Britain

Library of Congress Catalog Card No. 70–86905

Contents

Illustrations

Music Examples

Acknowledgements

In writing this book, my chief sources of information have been the authoritative biographies by Ursula Vaughan Williams and Michael Kennedy, published by the Oxford University Press. Mrs. Vaughan Williams has been unstinting in the personal help she has given—in reading and commenting upon my manuscript, in supplying photographic material, and in making known certain items of recently-discovered information (the new date, 1906, for the incidental music to *The Pilgrim's Progress* is one example).

Short quotations have been taken, for the most part, from Vaughan Williams's autobiographical sketch, now available in *National Music*. Roy Douglas's account of the composer's working methods first appeared in the Vaughan Williams commemorative issue of the Royal College of Music Magazine (Easter 1959), and is here reproduced by permission.

With the exception of the *Pastoral Symphony* and the unison song *Let us now praise famous men*, which are the copyright of J. Curwen & Sons, and the hymn-tune prelude *Rhosymedre*, which is published by Stainer & Bell, all the music examples are reproduced by kind permission of the Oxford University Press. The symphonies, *Job*, *Greensleeves* and *Rhosymedre* are quoted in piano reductions of my own devising.

The photograph facing page 49 (*above*) is the copyright of the Radio Times Hulton Picture Library. The composer's manuscripts are now lodged in the British Museum, where Department of Manuscripts made available the photographic reproductions used in this book.

Sincere apologies are offered to any person or body whose contribution to this book has been overlooked.

Vaughan Williams

I

First Steps

Some composers write masterpieces at seventeen. Others, at the same age, seem to be almost without talent. Some—the Mozarts of this world—cram a lifetime's work into a few brief years. Others grow to maturity slowly, and blossom only late in life.

Ralph Vaughan Williams was one such late-developer. Had he died at the same age as Mozart or Schubert his name would have been forgotten long ago. Fortunately he lived to a ripe old age, and his genius grew with the years.

He was born on 12th October 1872, at Down Ampney—a village near Cricklade in Gloucestershire, a stone's throw from the great unswerving road the Romans called Ermine Street. The passing years have brought few changes. Down Ampney is still very much as it was when the Vaughan Williams family first came to live at the vicarage.

There were three children (two boys and a girl), and Ralph was the youngest. For them the future must have seemed more than ordinarily promising. Both the Rev. Arthur Vaughan Williams and Margaret, his wife, were well-connected. Generations of successful lawyers made up his side of the family, while she was a daughter of the wealthy Josiah Wedgwood (grandson of the famous potter) and could count the great Charles Darwin among her uncles. Thus, there was money in the family, social position, culture and intelligence.

It was as well that the background was solid and dependable, for in 1875 the Rev. Arthur Vaughan Williams died. His widow did not have to face poverty as well as grief. She took the children and went to live with her father and sister in the comfort and security of her own childhood home: Leith Hill Place, near Dorking. Though Gloucestershire was his place of birth, Surrey was where Ralph Vaughan Williams grew up.

For a child, life in a large country mansion in Victorian times was not quite the fairy-tale it might seem. True, there were servants and fine linen, ample food, and prospects of the best education that money could buy. But there were also long dark corridors in the light of flickering candles, cold spacious rooms that no fire, however large, could heat. And there was, above all, the iron hand of strict Victorian discipline. Children were kept firmly in their place.

It was, nevertheless, a happy time. With his brother and sister for companions, Ralph Vaughan Williams played games and learned his lessons in the nursery. He was an ordinary, cheerful boy—quite unremarkable, except in his love of music.

The sound of the piano delighted him. As soon as he could walk he made for the open keyboard. When he was six he wrote his first piece of music: four whole bars, which he called *The Robin's Nest*. His Aunt Sophy was so impressed that she began to give him lessons in musical theory, using a book elaborately entitled:

The Child's Introduction to Thorough Bass in Conversations of a Fortnight between a Mother and her Daughter aged Ten years old: London, printed for Baldwin Cradock and Joy, 14, Paternoster Row, 1819.

The 'conversations' are models of sober instruction, from which it may be supposed even a little boy might learn. Here, for example, is conversation 8:

MARY: Mama, have I anything more to learn about the chord of the 7th?

MOTHER: Yes, you already know how a simple chord of the 7th is formed, but you are also to learn that there are four different kinds of 7th.

There soon followed lessons in playing the piano; and then violin lessons with 'a wizened old German called Cramer'. By the time he was eight, Ralph Vaughan Williams felt confident enough to undertake a correspondence course in musical theory, organized by Edinburgh University. And though his Aunt Sophy had to help him make a fair copy of his answers (his own handwriting was difficult to read, even in those days) he had the satisfaction of passing two examinations with flying colours.

Such studies were a great help, especially when it came to writing music for the toy theatre which he shared with his brother and sister. A little book of *Overtures by Mr. R. V. Williams* still exists to tell us about such early masterpieces as *The Galoshes of Happienes* and *The Ram Opera*, copied in a laborious, sprawling hand, and complete with such business-like warnings as: 'Ent. Sta. Hall', and 'this overture is copyright . . .'

First Steps

Nursery life came to an end in 1883, when, following in his brother's footsteps, Ralph Vaughan Williams went to a preparatory school: Field House, Rottingdean. But the change did not bring an end to music-making. Violin and piano lessons continued, and there was at least one memorable visit to Brighton to hear a real orchestra play under the great Hans Richter.

He also discovered that music could make him famous—both with the boys, when he played his violin at night in the dormitory and set them 'dancing in their shirts', and with their parents, when he played Raff's *Cavatina* at the school concert.

Prep-school life in turn gave way to a public school: Charterhouse. Here, despite a typically nineteenth-century preoccupation with Latin and invigorating sports, he found that music was 'mildly encouraged'. There was a choir and a school orchestra, and the chance to play chamber music. Soon he asked leave to give a concert of his own devising in the school hall. The authorities, astonished but amused, gave their consent and, when it came to it, even patronized the event. The programme for 5th August 1888 included what is probably the first public performance of a Vaughan Williams work: a Trio in G, sitting proudly and confidently alongside music by Sullivan and Spohr. After the concert was over the excited composer had the pleasure of hearing what in later years he was to describe as 'one of the few words of encouragement I ever received in my life'. The mathematics master sought him out, and in solemn tones said: 'Very good, Williams. You must go on.'

In fact, he had every intention of going on. When the time came to leave Charterhouse and the question of choosing a career arose, he told his mother that music was all he cared for and that he wished to earn his living by playing in an orchestra.

The thought of a professional musician in the family was not entirely pleasant, however. Victorian England offered few opportunities for a successful career in music, and musicians, as a class, commanded little respect. It was a matter for serious discussion. Uncles and aunts were consulted. Heads were shaken, and eyes looked grave. At last it was decided that the only possible solution was for the boy to become a church organist. If he proved good enough he would at least be able to earn a living.

There was no point in arguing. It was a step in the right direction. And so, in the summer of 1890, Ralph Vaughan Williams left school, knowing that after the summer holidays he would go to London and the Royal College of Music, and that there his career would begin in earnest.

II

The Student

The two years that Ralph Vaughan Williams now spent at the Royal College mark the beginning of a musical education that was to last, on and off, until 1908. Few great composers have ever felt the need for so long and so thorough an apprenticeship; and fewer still would have had the patience to undergo the ordeal.

It was not as if he had the encouragement of being obviously brilliant. For the most part his teachers shook their heads and sighed. If he persisted in writing music they would do their best to help him. With luck he might learn to write a few passable trifles. But they were firm on one point: he would never achieve anything great or lasting.

Fortunately he seems to have had an inner faith that nothing could shake. He knew that he would one day do something worthwhile; it was only a matter of finding the right road to travel on. And to his way of thinking, the right road did not include spending all day in the organ loft. He practised of course, for the problems of organ playing were not without interest, and the sound was grand. But he could not bring his whole heart to the matter. He did not feel like an organist, he felt like a composer.

By the end of his second term at the Royal College, Vaughan Williams had made such good progress in harmony and counterpoint that he was allowed to have his way. He joined Parry's composition class.

Hubert Parry was already one of the great names in English music. His choral ode *Blest Pair of Sirens* (1887) is still regarded as a landmark in the gradual revival of English musical genius that began to show itself in the second half of the nineteenth century, and it is easy to see why an aspiring young composer might feel it an honour to study with him. Parry was just the kind of teacher Vaughan Williams needed. He examined his 'horrible little songs and anthems' with scrupulous care. He was not content merely to point out the mistakes, but took endless pains to show how nonsense might be turned into acceptable music. When he realized how limited his pupil's

20

Ralph Vaughan Williams aged thirteen

Two early photographs of his parents

'The Galoshes of Happienes', an early attempt at composition

Down Ampney Vicarage, Vaughan Williams's birthplace

A rough draft entitled *Bushes and Briars*, 1903

experience had been ('Parry could hardly believe I knew so little music'), he set about finding remedies for the situation. He loaned him orchestral full-scores, played through Beethoven sonatas, sent him to concerts and questioned him closely on his reactions to the music he was now discovering. By sheer force of example, Parry began to turn Vaughan Williams into a musician.

The two years passed quickly, and soon the time to leave drew near. But the question of earning a living did not arise, for the family had decided that he should now complete the gentlemanly side of his education by going up to Cambridge. He was to read for a degree in History, and then, if he wished, take his Bachelor of Music degree.

The following years at Trinity College were a great delight. Not only were there friends and relations scattered throughout the University, but there were also musicians, both amateur and professional, on every hand. He worked hard: cramming for his music degree with Charles Wood, keeping up his organ practice with Alan Gray, and making quick dashes to London for composition lessons with Parry. At the same time he attended history lectures. In due course he obtained both the degrees he needed.

Most men would have been content. But Vaughan Williams still felt there was more to be learned. In 1895 he returned to the Royal College, this time to study with Sir Charles Stanford.

Lessons with Stanford were not an unqualified success. In later years, Vaughan Williams recalled:

'The details of my work annoyed Stanford so much that we seldom arrived at the broader issues and the lesson usually started with a conversation on these lines: "Damnably ugly, my boy, why do you write such things?" "Because I like them." "But you can't like them, they're not music." "I shouldn't write them if I didn't like them." So the argument went on and there was no time left for any constructive criticism.'

He then goes on to point out that Stanford's deeds were better than his words, and that he was always ready to back his pupil's music when it came to arranging a performance.

Vaughan Williams's final period at the Royal College was, nevertheless, to prove all-important. It was not so much the professors, helpful and stimulating though they were. It was the other students. And in 1895 Stanford was teaching composition to a particularly lively bunch.

Among them was Gustav von Holst—who, despite his name, also came from Gloucestershire. He was quite different from Vaughan Williams, both in character and background. There had been musicians in the Holst family for many generations—performers, teachers, and minor composers. Gustav's great-grandfather, born in Sweden, had settled in England at the beginning of the nineteenth century, and by now the only un-English thing about the family was the 'von' in their name (wisely, they dropped this when England declared war on Germany in 1914). They lived in Cheltenham, where Gustav's father was much respected as a teacher of the pianoforte. Gustav himself, however, had to fight hard to be allowed to study composition, for his father could see no future in a musical career that did not revolve round teaching. He was twenty before he arrived at the Royal College, desperately poor, but full of enthusiasm and with the advantage of a considerable practical experience of music-making behind him.

The difference between the young Holst and the young Vaughan Williams could scarcely have been greater. Yet they struck up an immediate friendship and, to all intents and purposes, began to teach each other. They talked about everything under the sun and music in particular. They criticized each other's work with cheerful severity. At the same time they urged each other on. In some obscure way they both felt that the future of English music lay in their hands.

So greatly did they value each other's criticism, that they continued what they called their 'field days' long after they had both been accepted by the world as important composers. Indeed, only the untimely death of Gustav Holst brought their relationship to an end. Few friendships between great composers have proved so fruitful.

The year of his return to the Royal College also saw Ralph Vaughan Williams in his first professional post. It was as respectable as the family could have wished. He was appointed organist to the church of St. Barnabas, South Lambeth, at a salary of £50 a year.

He was not the best organist the world has ever known, nor was he particularly happy in the job. But at least he was making music in a practical way, and he found the experience invaluable. Thus encouraged he went on to found a choral society and a small orchestra. Both were 'pretty bad', according to his own account, but they were decidedly useful to a budding composer—better, in fact, than all the text-book degrees in the world.

Vaughan Williams's second and final period at the Royal College lasted until the summer of 1897. He left, having made two important decisions: first, to marry; and second, to spend at least a few months studying in Germany.

Of the two, marriage was probably the easier to accomplish. He knew

Thanks awfully for the photograph...

An early letter from Vaughan Williams to Holst, _c._ 1895

precisely who his wife was to be. He had met her at Cambridge. She was beautiful, intelligent, and an accomplished amateur musician. Her name was Adeline Fisher; and when, eventually, she accepted him, both families declared themselves delighted at the match. They married in October 1897, and set out for a honeymoon in Berlin.

Once there, after the first flurry of sight-seeing and concert-going, he settled down to several months of hard work as a pupil of Max Bruch at the famous Hochschule für Musik.

Even after they had returned to London in the following year, the process of musical education was to continue. He sat for his F.R.C.O. diploma, and then for his Doctorate at Cambridge. By 1900, Ralph Vaughan Williams was, in terms of paper honours, as well-qualified a composer as ever set pen to paper.

But he had still not discovered a musical voice of his own. He had written a great deal of music, and some of it had attracted favourable comment—songs such as 'Linden Lea' and 'Silent Noon' date from this period. Yet there was something missing. Any one of a dozen composers might have put their names to what he had so far produced. There was little to suggest that a new and highly individual talent was about to emerge.

'Why not try looking-glass music? This took me ¼ hour!'
Vaughan Williams in a letter to Gustav Holst, *c*. 1897.

III

The Folksong Collector

From 1902 Vaughan Williams gave regular lectures in and around London, as part of the university scheme for adult education. His subject was *Folksong*. At the end of one such lecture, at Brentwood in Essex, two old ladies suggested he might like to come to a Parish Tea which they were helping to arrange at the nearby village of Ingrave. They felt sure that the villagers would remember some of the old songs and be only too happy to sing them. Though he was a little doubtful, Vaughan Williams eventually agreed to go.

When it came to it, nobody sang at the tea party. One old man, Charles Pottipher, a shepherd who had lived all his life at Ingrave, was asked and asked again. Each time he refused. He knew songs, of course, and he wasn't ashamed of his voice, but the Vicar's tea party was not the place for such recitals. If the gentleman from London would like to visit him in his own home, that would be another matter.

Vaughan Williams agreed, and next day, 4th December 1903, more out of politeness than anything else, he knocked on Mr. Pottipher's door. No longer in his best clothes or on his best behaviour, Mr. Pottipher was a different man. He sat his guest down, opened his mouth and began to sing:

> *Through bushes and through briars*
> *As I lately took my way*
> *All for to hear the small birds sing*
> *And the lambs to skip and play.*

He sang his song over and over, until every note and every word had been safely written down.

Without knowing it, Mr. Pottipher had changed the course of Vaughan Williams's life. Ideas that had long been simmering just below the surface now began to assume the utmost importance. English folksong was no longer something to be read about in a book. It was alive and all around him. It was, moreover, the kind of music to which he responded with his whole heart.

Nowadays some people find it fashionable to sneer at folksong, to lump it in with hand-weaving and basket-making and all the thousand and one crafts that modern machinery has made redundant. But its importance for certain composers (Bartók and Kodály in Hungary, for example; Janáček in Czechoslovakia) can scarcely be overestimated. In each case, the discovery of his country's folksong liberated the composer from the deadweight of an alien tradition. Through folksong he arrived at a kind of musical speech which was as natural as his native language, and through which he could express not only his own individuality, but the individuality of his country.

So it was with Vaughan Williams. Imagine what it must have been like for an English composer at the beginning of the twentieth century. You would have known that the great line of English composers had come to an end in 1695, with the death of Henry Purcell. During the eighteenth and nineteenth centuries the outlook had been very bleak: no one to match Bach or Handel, Haydn or Mozart, Beethoven or Wagner. You could be forgiven if you had come to believe that the only music worth trying to write was music in the German style.

And this, indeed, was what happened to Elgar. English musical genius came fully to life again in his music. He was a great composer, able to stand comparison with any of his contemporaries—German, French, or Italian. But he was a composer in the German manner, none the less.

Of course, it did not matter. The German style suited Elgar. He could borrow from it and still be original. But for Vaughan Williams it was all wrong. To him the German manner was a foreign language: he could speak it, but it did not come naturally. What he needed was a kind of musical speech that was truly English.

Folksong pointed the way. He soaked himself in its melodic shapes and peculiar rhythms. Little by little his music took colour from them, and in doing so gave an outlet to his own kind of originality.

The reason why folksong has had such an influence on certain composers is simple to explain. Folksong is closely related to language. In most cases the words and music cannot be thought of separately, for they come into existence at one and the same time. They are invented by ordinary men and women for their own pleasure. Nobody writes them down. They are handed from father to son, village to village, country to country, and age to age. They are changed and polished by countless singers, through many generations. But they always remain a direct and accurate reflection of the language that gave them birth.

Take any sentence in the English language, translate it into French and you will find that its rhythm and sound are completely changed: each suggests a quite different melody. Translate the same sentence into German or Italian, or any language that takes your fancy, and the same thing happens. Each language has its own natural rhythms and its own internal melody. It would seem likely that these patterns correspond to something fundamental in the people who speak the language.

Any composer who cares to take a hint from his country's folksong will, inevitably, learn something about the character of his fellow-countrymen and the kind of musical expression that comes naturally to them. He may also learn something about himself.

Armed with a handful of notebooks and a pocket full of pencils, Vaughan Williams began his search for English folksong. During the next ten years he noted down more than 800 examples—some good, some quite ordinary, and some that were overwhelmingly beautiful.

'My Coffin Shall be Black': sung by Mr. Kinnaird

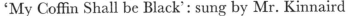

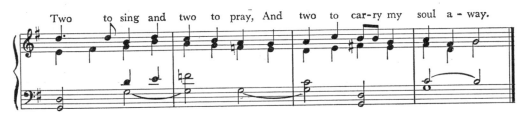

He was not the only enthusiast. Cecil Sharp, for example, was his friendly rival and colleague. He had come to folksong when, in searching for suitable material to use in singing classes, he had begun to explore the rather spare collections of 'national' songs that had been published during the nineteenth century. In 1899 he came across a group of Morris Dancers at Headington in Oxfordshire, and in 1903 collected his first folksong ('The Seeds of Love') when he overheard an old gardener singing to himself as he mowed a lawn.

From then on, folksong became his life's work, and he pursued it both in England and America.

The folksong collectors were only just in time. Towns were swallowing up the countryside and destroying traditional ways of life. Young people no longer felt obliged to stay in the same village and do as their fathers had done. Least of all were they inclined to sing the old songs and tell the old stories. Soon the gramophone and the radio would squeeze everybody's tastes into the same mould. But even before that final indignity the change was almost complete: for the Great War of 1914–18 shattered the structure

Sine Nomine: English Hymnal No. 641

In moderate time (♩ = 112)

For all the Saints who from their la - bours rest,

Who thee by faith be - fore the world con - fest,

name, O Je - - su, be for ev - er blest. A - -

- lle - lu - - ya! A - - lle - lu - - ya!

Above, Vaughan Williams and his wife, Adeline, in about 1909;
below, Leith Hill Place, Surrey

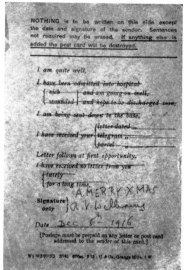

Left, Private Vaughan Williams in 1916; *right*, First World War letter-form
signed by Vaughan Williams; *below*, the White Gates, Dorking, 1929

of English society and swept the past and its simple pleasures into the history books. By 1918, the great days of folksong collecting were at an end.

In 1904 it must have seemed to Vaughan Williams that everything was conspiring to force him to examine the grass-roots of English music. Not only was he fascinated by folksong, but he had been asked to prepare a hymn book to replace the old *Hymns Ancient & Modern*, and was therefore much concerned in the study of another aspect of national song.

He worked for two years on this project: scouring long-forgotten hymn books for fine tunes and appropriate words, writing tunes of his own, or asking his friends to. The result, the *English Hymnal*, is a masterly tribute to his skill and understanding. The five million and more copies that were sold during the first fifty years of its existence have helped to revolutionize the musical side of religion in England. Splendid tunes from all ages are matched with equally splendid words. And not least among the glories are Vaughan Williams's own contributions: such hymns as *Sine Nomine* (For all the Saints), *Down Ampney* (Come down, O Love Divine), and *Randolph* (God be with you till we meet again).

It takes a very special kind of composer to write simple tunes that can be sung again and again.

IV

A Taste of Success

Folksong began to have an almost immediate effect on the music Vaughan Williams was writing. A particularly fruitful visit to King's Lynn in January 1905, for example, prompted the first *Norfolk Rhapsody*. He had listened to sailors and fishermen and, over the course of three days, jotted down no fewer than forty songs. Some of these—'The Captain's Apprentice', 'A Bold Young Sailor', and 'On Board a Ninety-eight'—became the basis for his new orchestral work, and the result was at once unmistakably English in flavour and at the same time highly personal.

'A Bold Young Sailor': sung by Mr. Anderson
King's Lynn, Norfolk 10th January, 1905

A bold young sai - lor cour - ted me, And stole a -
way my lib - er - ty, He stole my heart with my
free ___ good - will, I must con - fess I love him still.

So deeply did Vaughan Williams absorb these experiences, that when he could not find originals to suit his purpose he found it easy to invent 'folksongs' of his own. The themes used in the orchestral piece *In the Fen Country*, for example, are entirely his invention, yet they sound like age-old tunes. For the first time in his life, Vaughan Williams was composing in a style which came absolutely naturally to him.

Although the music he wrote during this period was, for the most part, favourably received, it did not always please the composer. He disowned certain pieces altogether, destroying the manuscripts wherever he could. Others he subjected to endless revisions. *In the Fen Country*, for example, was revised not only in 1905 and 1907, but again in 1935. His capacity for self-criticism (quite different from self-doubt, by the way) verged almost upon mania. The more accomplished he became, the more it grew. He would brood over scores, and then, long after his publishers had thought them safely launched, suddenly come up with a string of alterations and improvements.

It was probably this feeling that he could always add something to his musical knowledge and understanding that led him to become the conductor of the Leith Hill Festival, which his sister Margaret had helped to found in 1905. The idea that village choirs should meet each year in friendly rivalry, and then combine in the performance of some great masterpiece appealed to him enormously. This, he felt, was what music was all about. Music was for people, and not for library shelves.

His choirs loved and respected him—even when, on rare occasions, something would provoke a flash of white-hot rage. He wrote works for them to sing, and directed their attention to works that deserved their singing. And when the festival was fully on its feet, he indulged himself and his choirs in memorable performances of the work he admired above all others: Bach's *St. Matthew Passion*.

By 1908 Vaughan Williams had become an established figure in English music. Physically it would have been impossible to ignore him, whatever his talents. He was tall (6ft. 1in.), big-boned and bulky. His hair was black and luxuriant, his eyes blue-grey. He was, by any standard, a very handsome man. Yet, however confident and commanding he may have appeared, he was, in himself, still far from sure. There was something in his music that displeased him. It was 'lumpy', he thought, and 'stodgy'—too Germanic by half. He had come to a dead end, and now needed some new musical experience if his work was to progress.

His thoughts turned to France: to the music of Maurice Ravel, and the idea of studying in Paris. He could scarcely have chosen a greater contrast to the kind of composer he had so far worked under. Ravel's wit and sophistication, his delight in orchestral glitter and surface decoration, the delicacy of his intricate melodic lines and the soft evasiveness of his harmonies seemed almost shocking after the heavy German earnestness that most English musicians still swore by. Paris fashions might well be fascinating, but, like everything else in that cheerful city, they were rather suspect.

The first lesson started badly. Ravel looked at the music he had brought,

A SEA SYMPHONY
by
R.V.W.

First Performance in London,
February 4th, 1913
By THE BACH CHOIR.

MENU.

Consommé Riche en Tasse

Filets de Sole Sévigné

Noisettes d'Agneau Grillées

Haricots Verts

Pommes Mignonnes

Cailles de Vigne Rôties

Salade

Ananas Princes

Friandises

"Princes."
Piccadilly W.   *4th February, 1913*

R.V.W.

SINFONIA ANTARTICA
by
R.V.W.

First Performance in London
21st January, 1953
By THE HALLÉ ORCHESTRA

MENU

Consommé Bouquetière

Canetons Rôtis aux Cerises
Pommes Rissolées
Petits Pois au Beurre

Pêche St. Georges

Fromage

Café

Royal Festival Hall Restaurant   *21st January, 1953*

and then, with a sigh, suggested he should write 'a little minuet in the style of Mozart'. Vaughan Williams was horrified. Summoning up his best French he replied that although he had given up his career and said goodbye to his friends in order to study in Paris, it was not to write '*un petit menuet dans le style de Mozart*'. After that they got along famously.

He remained in Paris for three months. On his return it was observed that his music now sounded as if he had been 'having tea with Debussy', and he himself admitted to 'a bad attack of French fever'. But whether or not his Paris venture was solely responsible for the change that now came over his music, one thing is certain: there was a change, and it marked a definite step forward. Three works of outstanding importance prove the point: the song-cycle *On Wenlock Edge* (1909), the *Sea Symphony* (1910), and the *Fantasia on a theme of Thomas Tallis*, also 1910.

For the song-cycle he chose poems by A. E. Housman, setting them for tenor, with string quartet and piano accompaniment. Housman's *Shropshire Lad* poems were, during this period and for many years to come, enormously popular with English composers and called forth a great many limp, pastoral settings. Vaughan Williams, however, went out of his way to underline their grim dramatic side, and produced a work which is virtually a miniature opera.

The *Sea Symphony*, a setting for chorus and orchestra of poems by the American Walt Whitman, is perhaps less remarkable. Vaughan Williams began work on it in 1903, at a time when no English composer had written a symphony of any importance (Elgar's first symphony was not performed until 1908). Even so, and despite the fact that it is a choral work, the *Sea Symphony* is truly symphonic in stature; and though the example of Parry, Stanford, Holst, and Elgar left many a mark on its pages, there is still enough of Vaughan Williams's own personality to bind it together as a coherent and effective piece. Broad and spacious in conception, it deals not only with the varying moods of the sea, but also with its symbolic, mystical significance for man. It is therefore one of the earliest of his works that prompts the listener to search for 'meanings'.

The unequivocal masterpiece, however, is the *Tallis Fantasia*. Here, German thoroughness is lightened by French sophistication, and English folk-song is absorbed into a personal style of great breadth and passion. From Tallis's noble tune, Vaughan Williams evolves far-reaching consequences—climaxes of enormous emotional and dramatic power. Scored for two string orchestras and a string quartet, the work exploits every device of massed and solo sound, echo and antiphony—effects admirably suited to performance in some great cathedral, as at the Gloucester Three Choirs Festival where it was first heard. On the strength of this work alone, Vaughan Williams's name would have lived.

Harmonisation of Tallis's Hymn-tune

But there was more to come. The success of the *Tallis Fantasia* led to further Three Choirs commissions: from Worcester for the following year (*Five Mystical Songs*), and then from Hereford for the year after that (*Fantasia on Christmas Carols*). At the same time, his delight in English folksong had led him to make sketches for a ballad-opera, *Hugh the Drover*. He was also busy with plans for a new symphony—this time for orchestra only.

In view of all the work he had on hand, it is not surprising that the new symphony took time to grow. Indeed, it was very nearly not a symphony at all—for Vaughan Williams's first ideas were for a tone-poem about London.

A Taste of Success

But it soon became obvious that what he had to say went far beyond the capacity of a tone-poem. What was emerging was *A London Symphony*.

Many foolish things have been said about Vaughan Williams: one of them being that he looked and behaved like a farmer, and was a dyed-in-the-wool countryman at heart. Certainly he enjoyed walking, but he was far from easy in the countryside. London was the place he loved best. London was his home, and, so far as he was concerned, he was a Londoner: just the man, in fact, to tackle the kind of work he now had in mind.

But, despite its origins, it would be wrong to regard *A London Symphony* as being in any way descriptive. In a programme-note written in 1920, Vaughan Williams made his own attitude perfectly clear:

> The title *A London Symphony* may suggest to some hearers a descriptive piece, but this is not the intention of the composer. A better title would perhaps be 'Symphony by a Londoner', that is to say, the life of London (including, possibly, its various sights and sounds) has suggested to the composer an attempt at musical expression; but it would be no help to the hearer to describe this in words. The music is intended to be self-expressive, and must stand or fall as 'absolute' music. Therefore, if listeners recognize suggestions of such things as the 'Westminster Chimes' or the 'Lavender Cry' they are asked to consider these as accidents, not essentials of the music.

Leaving aside the hints of cockney street-tunes and jingling horse-drawn cabs, the striking feature of *A London Symphony* is its power to turn, quite suddenly, into atmospheres of terror and foreboding. The impression of seeing, momentarily, beyond the comforts of everyday life into regions that are far from reassuring, is something which haunts nearly all Vaughan Williams's symphonies. Like all visions of any importance, they can be very frightening.

Rehearsals for the first performance began early in 1914. Vaughan Williams was nervous. He already had plans for tinkering with the score (he eventually made two major revisions: one in 1920 and one in 1933). He was far from certain how his first real symphony would be received. But on March 27th there was no doubting what the audience thought, or what his fellow musicians felt. Gustav Holst spoke for them all, when he wrote next day:

> You really have done it this time. Not only have you reached the heights, but you have taken your audience with you.

V

A World at War

The strange note of terror that intrudes upon the bustle and gaiety of *A London Symphony* was soon to find an echo in reality. On August 4th 1914, England was forced to declare war on Germany, and Europe was plunged into chaos.

Like many of his younger friends, Vaughan Williams immediately decided that he would volunteer for service. There was no need for him to do so. He was forty-two and in no danger of being conscripted. Army disciplines would be especially hard for a man of his age and upbringing. But he did not hesitate. In September 1914 he enlisted for service with the Royal Army Medical Corps and began his training.

Fortunately he was accustomed to walking—the years of folksong collecting had seen to that. And so, apart from the eternal problem of getting his puttees to stay in place and his cap to sit at the regulation angle, army life did not prove as bad as most people would have predicted for him. He settled in with men half his age and became their cheerful companion and friend.

Even his musical education came in handy. He was detailed to play the organ for church parades, and promptly amused himself and his comrades by improvising variations on the popular song 'Make Up Your Mind Maggie McKenzie' as a voluntary. And sometimes he was able to gather together a small choir to sing carols and folksongs.

In due course he was sent to France and the starker realities of war. Strange as it may seem, the sound of gunfire did not drive all thoughts of music out of his head. Ideas for a new symphony began to take shape, and the noise of battle helped to shape them. Though not completed until 1922, the *Pastoral Symphony* was a direct outcome of his wartime experience. It is not, as he later pointed out, 'lambkins frisking, as most people take for granted', but much more the song of a soldier far from home and thinking of a landscape he loves.

The Pastoral Symphony: fourth movement

And if this symphony is also shot through with desolation and terror, that too may be attributed to war. By 1916 Vaughan Williams had reason enough for sadness. He wrote to his friend Holst:

'I sometimes dread coming back to normal life with so many gaps—especially of course George Butterworth—he has left most of his MS to me —& now I hear that Ellis is killed—out of those seven who joined up together in August 1914 only three are left—I sometimes think now that it is wrong to have made friends with people much younger than oneself—because soon there will only be the middle aged left—& I have got out of touch with most of my contemporary friends—but there is always you & thank Heaven we have never got out of touch & I don't see why we ever should.'

QUEEN'S HALL

Sole Lessees—Messrs. CHAPPELL & Co., LTD.

27th SEASON, 1922-23.

SATURDAY, FEB. 10TH, 1923,
AT 3 O'CLOCK.

SOLO PIANOFORTE—
NIKISCH.

THE NEW
QUEEN'S HALL ORCHESTRA
(Proprietors—Messrs. CHAPPELL & Co., LTD.
PRIN. VIOLIN · MR. MAURICE SONS
ORGANIST · DR. STANLEY MARCHANT

CONDUCTORS
SIR HENRY J. WOOD
AND
DR. R. VAUGHAN WILLIAMS

SYMPHONY CONCERTS

FRANK NVDD

ANALYTICAL PROGRAMME, ONE SHILLING.

Programme for a concert given at Queen's Hall and conducted by Vaughan Williams

He did not stay long in France. Shortly before the end of 1916 his unit was moved to a secret destination—but not before a postcard bearing a Dorian scale had slipped past the censor unremarked, to tell his wife and friends that he was now on his way to Greece. Later he was able to give them the improbable news that his choir had sung Christmas carols standing on the slopes of Mount Olympus itself.

In 1917 the army suddenly decided that a man of Vaughan Williams's background and education ought, by rights, to be an officer and promptly made arrangements to return him to England for the necessary training. He reached London in record time—simply because the officer in charge of his transfer had fallen from his horse and been taken delirious into hospital muttering, over and over again, 'We must do something about Vaughan Williams,' until everybody was convinced that the eventual outcome of the war was somehow bound up with this particular soldier's welfare.

For his own part, he was far from happy at this new turn of events. He disliked the convention that divided soldiers into 'officers' and 'men', and generally let it be known which he thought was the more honourable title. The army, however, was not disposed to understand his point of view, and to England he went.

As an officer in the Royal Garrison Artillery, Vaughan Williams spent the last year of the war in France. This time he was posted to Rouen and, as a graceful tribute to his new rank, placed in sole command of two hundred horses. He remained in France until the Armistice was signed.

Since the army could not demobilise all its troops at the same time, it took the sensible step of providing them with opportunities for education and entertainment. Vaughan Williams was relieved of his regimental duties, and now found himself Director of Music, First Army, B.E.F., France—charged with drumming up choirs, orchestras, and anything else that might seem useful in the circumstances. By the time he himself was ready to say goodbye to army life, in February 1919, he had founded nine choral societies, three music-classes, an orchestra, and a military band.

VI

Promise and Achievement

Ralph Vaughan Williams was forty-seven when he returned to civilian life. He was no longer the bouncing, youthful figure that most people mean when they speak of a 'promising composer'; yet in terms of actual achievement this was what he was. The war had robbed him of four vital years; and apart from a handful of ideas which might or might not knit together into a convincing symphony, it had given very little in return. Perhaps he would not be able to pick up the threads of his creative life. Perhaps he would simply settle down to a peaceful middle-age, teaching, writing the occasional uneventful work, and generally behaving in the time-honoured manner of the 'safe' English composer. Almost anything was possible.

The immediate problem of making a fresh start was solved when, together with Gustav Holst, he was appointed to teach composition at the Royal College. He was never, in the strict sense of the word, a great teacher —creative geniuses are seldom that. But he had an open mind and a genuine desire to help, and was quite ungrudging in the amount of time he was prepared to devote to a worthwhile pupil. One famous piece of advice sums up his attitude to composing, and the attitude he liked to encourage as a teacher:

> Never try to be original. If you are original you needn't try. If you aren't, no amount of trying will make you so.

His pupils repaid him with loyalty and devotion, many of them returning for advice and encouragement long after they had themselves become famous.

In the meantime he had his own work to attend to. First there were the sketches for the *Pastoral Symphony* to be brooded over and moulded into shape. This occupied him for several years. His habit of working at several major pieces at once made progress look slower than it actually was. Even-

A piano-duet version of the second movement of the Fourth Symphony

tually a number of new works would emerge in quick succession, and then the sheer volume of his industry would be apparent.

While working on the *Pastoral Symphony*, he was also occupied with the Mass in G minor for unaccompanied choir which was eventually performed in 1922; a one-act opera based on an episode from John Bunyan's *The Pilgrim's Progress from This World to That Which is to Come*, which he called *The Shepherds of the Delectable Mountains* (1922) a rhapsody for violin and orchestra, *The Lark Ascending* (1920); and the ballet *Old King Cole* (1923).

The Bunyan opera provides an excellent illustration of the way certain ideas lingered in Vaughan Williams's mind for many years. He had composed music for a stage version of Bunyan's book as early as 1906. A few bars of this found fuller expression in *The Shepherds of the Delectable Mountains*, which was itself incorporated bodily into the full-scale opera-morality *The Pilgrim's Progress*—the composition of which occupied him, on and off, from 1922 to 1952. His creative life can thus be seen to be all of a piece. Buoyed up by patience and tenacity, it was simply a matter of allowing his ideas to ripen in their own good time. And then the masterpiece would emerge.

His habit of storing away musical ideas which he felt he had not yet used to the best advantage is another aspect of the same process. Years later he would find that he could return to these ideas and make something really worthwhile of them. An example occurs in an incomplete and now totally forgotten orchestral work which was to have been called *In the New Forest*. Two movements were actually performed in 1903, and one of them contained the following idea:

'The Solent': second movement of
Four Impressions for Orchestra
In the New Forest

The same idea crops up in music he wrote for the film *The England of Elizabeth* (1955); and again, more gloriously, in the second movement of the Ninth Symphony (1957):

Symphony No. 9: second movement

Promise and Achievement

It is no exaggeration to say that one of the hall-marks of great art is precisely this sense of unity and coherence in the artist's life. Everything travels in the same direction.

In certain cases, however, the long delay between the first idea for a new work and its actual appearance before the public, merely reflects the difficulty of finding the proper occasion for a performance. This is particularly true of Vaughan Williams's operas, all of which have suffered from the English reluctance to believe that any English composer could ever write an opera of real value. It was left to the Royal College of Music to give the first performances of *Hugh the Drover*—the ballad-opera which Vaughan Williams wrote between 1910 and 1914. A professional performance, by the British National Opera Company, followed in the same year (1924).

Encouraged by the reception, and by the fact that English opera seemed to have taken on a new lease of life (Rutland Boughton's *The Immortal Hour* was at the height of its success, and the BNOC had already produced Holst's *The Perfect Fool*), Vaughan Williams began work on a full-length opera, *Sir John in Love*. He did not complete the score until 1928, and by that time the English opera revival had fizzled out. *Sir John in Love* remained condemned to amateur performances until the Sadler's Wells production in 1946.

In such circumstances it is astonishing that Vaughan Williams was ever tempted to write opera again. But he was—on three occasions, and one of them, the one-act *Riders to the Sea*, composed between 1925 and 1932 and first performed in 1937, was to rank as one of the few great masterpieces of English opera.

Besides a string of important new works (the oratorio *Sancta Civitas*, and the *Concerto Accademico* in 1925, and *Flos Campi* in the following year), the twenties brought Vaughan Williams various personal adventures. In 1922, for example, he went to America for the first time. As guests of the wealthy music-lover Carl Stoeckel, he and his wife received every attention and could scarcely have enjoyed themselves more—even though by the end of the trip he had begun to mutter darkly that he could now understand how Mozart and his contemporaries felt living under a patron.

Less immediately exciting, but of more lasting importance, was his meeting, in 1924, with the newly established music publishing department of the Oxford University Press. Hubert Foss, the man in charge, soon became his close friend and trusted adviser. In him he found the ideal publisher: imaginative, scholarly, business-like, and, above all, someone who really understood and believed in his music. 'Ask Foss about it' became one of Vaughan Williams's daily sayings. With O.U.P. as his sole publishers, his

Riders to the Sea : closing scene

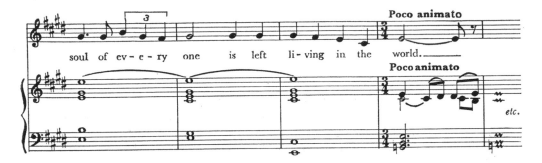

soul of ev - e - ry one is left li - ving in the world.

career began to prosper; while, in turn, his music helped to establish them as an important music-publishing house.

Had he felt gloomy during these years, however, it would not have been surprising. With such lyrical, folksong-inspired works as *Sir John in Love* still falling from his pen, he was beginning to look a trifle old-fashioned. An established English composer, living comfortably in a rambling eccentric house in Dorking (he left his London home in Cheyne Walk and moved to 'The White Gates' in 1929)—was there anything new to be expected of such a man?

But there were straws in the wind, if you knew where to look. The ballet *Job*, begun in 1927 and first performed as a concert piece at Norwich in 1930 and as a stage work in London during the following year, was not quite orthodox Vaughan Williams. Based on Blake's visionary illustrations to *The Book of Job*, it was a work that underlined the very personal religious quality of his music, and at the same time hinted at turbulent passions beneath the surface. There was a leanness and angularity about this new work that caused some critics to wonder if they had not been a little premature in judging their man.

By the middle of 1934, however, champions of British music were in no position to argue about Vaughan Williams's presumed stature. He was suddenly and cruelly thrust into the front rank of English composers—not by any achievement of his own, but by the simple facts of death. For in 1934, Elgar, Delius, and, hardest of all to bear, his friend Gustav Holst died. Ralph Vaughan Williams was now the senior English composer. The only other man of undisputed genius, William Walton, was his junior by thirty years!

From *Sir John in Love*: Fantasia on Greensleeves

Job: 'Saraband of the Sons of God'

Andante con moto ($\dot{} = 80$)

VII

The Acknowledged Master

In all the arts, the business of being astonishing and provocative is generally left to young men. The mature artist—the sixty-two-year-old composer, say—is apt to proceed along more predictable lines: consolidating the revolutions with which he startled the world as a youth, bringing his creative life to its conclusion with some mellow swan song of infinite wisdom and serenity. The announcement that Vaughan Williams's Fourth Symphony would receive its first performance on 10th April 1935, might reasonably have been thought to herald just such a tranquil last period.

Leith Hill Place, 1947, from a drawing by Barbara Allen

48

Above, Vaughan Williams with Lady Allen Hurtwood, E. M. Forster and the Band-master at Abinger in July 1934; *below*, Vaughan Williams conducting a rehearsal of *England's Pleasant Land* at Milton Court, Wescott, July 1938

Above, conducting a Promenade Concert performance of *A London Symphony* in 1946; *below*, Vaughan Williams with his second wife, Ursula, and Sir John Barbirolli during a rehearsal of *A Sea Symphony* in Manchester, 1951

The Acknowledged Master

But the new symphony did not conform to expectations. It was as bold and aggressive as the music of any determined young modernist. The harsh, uncompromising dissonance of the opening bars had brilliantly set the pace for what followed: a work of blunt severity—a reflection, as some were later to think, of the political unrest in Europe that was already sowing the seeds of a second world war.

There seems to have been no special reason why Vaughan Williams's genius should suddenly have taken this turn. His personal life was still placid and unremarkable. There was no indication that he had reached any cross-road, either as an artist or a man. His powers had simply and unexpectedly

Symphony No. 4: first movement

come into full focus. He was in complete command: he knew what he wanted to say, and knew exactly how to say it.

Leaving on one side most of the works during the next two dozen years— some of them masterpieces, like the choral *Dona Nobis Pacem* (1936) and the *Serenade to Music* (1938); some of them comparative failures, like the comic opera *The Poisoned Kiss* (1936)—the really important achievements are the symphonies and the opera *The Pilgrim's Progress*.

He wrote five symphonies after 1935. Each is quite different in character, and each appeared just at the moment when the musical world had decided that he must at last have retired. Of these, the Fifth Symphony (1943) and the Sixth (1948) are outstanding, and together with the *Pastoral* and the Fourth they form the crown of his achievement as a composer.

But whereas the Fourth Symphony is harsh and dissonant, the Fifth is calm and serene. It is almost as if Vaughan Williams wished to offer comfort and peace to a stricken world—for this symphony was written during the blackest days of the Second World War. The fact that he used some of the themes in *The Pilgrim's Progress* only serves to underline the kind of meaning the symphony may be supposed to have.

Symphony No. 5: first movement

THE DORKING AND LEITH HILL DISTRICT
PRESERVATION SOCIETY PRESENT

ENGLAND'S PLEASANT LAND

A PAGEANT PLAY

Written by
E. M. FORSTER

Music directed by
R. VAUGHAN WILLIAMS

Composers
WILLIAM COLE
MARY COUPER
D. MOULE EVANS
JULIAN GARDINER
JOHN TICEHURST
R. VAUGHAN WILLIAMS

PRODUCED BY TOM HARRISON

MILTON COURT, WESTCOTT, SURREY
(By kind permission of Lady Mallaby-Deeley)
JULY 9TH, 14TH AND 16TH, 1938

The Acknowledged Master

With the Sixth Symphony, however, Vaughan Williams appeared to turn his back on hope and consolation. It was now 1948. The first atomic bombs had been dropped. He had lived through two world wars, and there was talk of a third. Many listeners saw in his symphony a cry of protest and despair.

What these remarkable works may mean is ultimately a matter that the

Symphony No. 6: fourth movement

individual must decide for himself. Vaughan Williams made a point of denying any specific interpretation. 'I feel angry with certain critics,' he wrote, 'who will have it that my Fourth Symphony "means" war, and that my Fifth "means" peace.' But faced with music of such power, it is impossible not to wonder about meanings.

Vaughan Williams's last three symphonies, though less immediately impressive, are also highly individual. The Eighth Symphony (1956) is full of good humour and inventive surprise, with the composer revelling in unusual orchestral sounds. The Ninth (1958) is more sombre and menacing. There is nothing in either symphony to suggest that Vaughan Williams was now in his eighties. The Eighth, in fact, is so light and playful, so bubbling with invention, that it could easily be the work of a very young man.

The seventh of Vaughan Williams's nine symphonies has a title: *Sinfonia Antartica*. It was completed in 1952 and draws its thematic material from the music that he wrote in 1948 for the film *Scott of the Antarctic*. Despite moments of grandeur and great beauty, the symphony has never been wholly accepted. Perhaps its connection with the film world is a little too obvious.

Though it seems fairly easy to decide which of the symphonies are masterpieces, it is almost impossible to reach any very convincing conclusions about *The Pilgrim's Progress*. To begin with, it is not quite an opera. Vaughan Williams was careful to call it 'a morality', but was equally insistent that its place was in the theatre. It was not to be treated as some kind of oratorio.

But what opera house can do justice to 'a morality'? Certainly not Covent Garden, where it received its first performance in April 1951. The crimson and gold of the splendid auditorium seemed completely out of touch with the Puritan severity of Bunyan's tale and the restrained ecstasy of Vaughan Williams's music. The visions that the Fifth Symphony can conjure up in even the least imaginative mind, seemed tawdry and laughable when transferred to paint and canvas and the all-too solid reality of the opera singer. Not surprisingly, the work was pronounced a noble failure, and the composer was bitterly hurt.

Nevertheless, this work, which occupied his thoughts for so many years, must be judged in company with his finest symphonies. For one thing, it raises the whole question of his attitude to religion. At Cambridge he declared himself an atheist, but in later years it would have been more accurate to describe him as an agnostic. Though he could not swallow church dogma, his whole nature was deeply religious. He responded wholeheartedly to the language of the Bible and the great mystical poets, and, in his music, sought to express a similar order of religious truth.

The Pilgrim's Progress : Act IV scene 1

And when thou com — — est thi - ther thou may-est see the gates of the Ce - les - — - tial Ci - ty.

It would be quite wrong to give the impression that Vaughan Williams existed on a plane of permanent mystical ecstasy. He was more than capable of holding his own in the market places of music—as his dealings with the film world prove. The fact that he took to writing for this medium came as something of a surprise, even to his friends. He was, after all, sixty-eight when he tackled his first film score, *The 49th Parallel*.

Writing film music is generally considered a young man's job. There is no time for inspiration. The composer must work out his score to the last split-second. His music must change mood as swiftly as the film and as often. He must be ready to make radical changes, should the director require it. He must be prepared to find convincing music for every situation under the sun— situations which he may never have come face to face with, even in his wildest

55

dreams. And, usually, he is allowed a mere handful of days to complete his work.

Vaughan Williams plunged into the hectic world of film-making with all the relish of a schoolboy. He dropped his old habit of brooding over a score and simply got on with the job. 'It is extraordinary,' he wrote, 'how, under the pressure of necessity, a dozen or so bars in the middle of a movement are discovered to be redundant, how a fortissimo climax really ought to be a pianissimo fade-out.'

Later, and rather more wickedly, he recorded his opinion, for the benefit of young composers, that 'you must not be horrified if you find that a passage which you intended to portray the villain's mad revenge has been used by the musical director to illustrate the cats being driven out of the dairy. The truth is that within certain limits any music can be made to fit any situation.'

He went on writing film music to the end of his life, enjoying the task immensely. So far as he was concerned it was just another job that any composer should be ready to do. To him, the whole business of composing went hand-in-hand with making yourself useful to your fellow citizens. A symphony for a great orchestra, or a hymn-tune for the village choir: it was all the same—you did your best, nothing less was good enough.

Curiously, it was this very willingness to be useful that led some critics to see in Vaughan Williams little more than an inspired amateur, stumbling, from time to time, upon original thoughts. In some ways he played up to the idea—publicly accusing himself of having 'an amateurish technique'; remarking on such works as the Fourth Symphony: 'I don't know whether I like it, but this is what I meant'; or writing jocular programme notes, designed to puncture the pompous cleverness of professional musical analysts. His comments on the Sixth Symphony, for example:

When the episode is over, the woodwind experiment as to how the fugue subject will sound upside down but the brass are angry and insist on playing it the right way up, so for a bit the two go on together and to the delight of everyone including the composer the two versions fit, so there is nothing to do now but to continue, getting more excited till the episode comes back very loud and twice as slow.

There was also the matter of his cheerful admission of 'cribbing' from other composers. He stated, for example, that the idea for Satan's Dance in *Job* sprang from the second movement of Beethoven's last quartet.

The connection is clear, but the outcome is totally different. The one is Beethoven, the other Vaughan Williams.

56

Job: 'Satan's Dance of Triumph'

Beethoven: String Quartet in F major, Op. 135: second movement

Opening bars

Bars 143-147

There never has been a composer who did not borrow, either consciously or unconsciously, from the music of other men. Few, however, have been willing to run the risk that Vaughan Williams took in admitting the fact.

ROYAL OPERA HOUSE

COVENT GARDEN

THURSDAY, 26th APRIL, 1951

THE ROYAL OPERA HOUSE, COVENT GARDEN LTD.

General Administrator: DAVID L. WEBSTER

presents

The first performance of

"THE PILGRIM'S PROGRESS"

A Morality in a Prologue, Four Acts and an Epilogue
founded on BUNYAN's ALLEGORY of the same name

Music by
RALPH VAUGHAN WILLIAMS, O.M.
(by arrangement with the Oxford University Press)

Scenery and Costumes by Hal Burton

CONDUCTOR : LEONARD HANCOCK

PRODUCER : NEVILL COGHILL

Programme for the premier of *The Pilgrim's Progress*, 1951

VIII

Last Years

A producer looking for someone to play the part of the Grand Old Man of English Music would have seized upon Vaughan Williams without hesitation. There he was, a bulky, untidy figure, with a face that managed to be both rugged and purposeful, and yet gentle and self-absorbed. He was to be seen wherever music had a part to play. In the concert-hall: encumbered, as time went on, with an increasingly strange assortment of hearing-aids, he listened intently to performances of his own music, or to the work of younger colleagues. He sat on wearisome committees and did battle to help neglected music and young composers. He made himself available to all who might need his help. He became, in short, a national figure, loved by musician and layman alike. V.W.—it was as simple as that.

Honours, of course, he might have had. But when asked, he made it clear that he did not wish to be crowned Master of the King's Musick (he would have followed Elgar), nor be buried alive under some grand title. 'Plain Mr. . . . Dr., if you prefer it', was as much as he could bear. He made only one exception to this rule, and that was in 1935, when the King offered him the Order of Merit. This, he felt, was too personal and too meaningful an honour to refuse.

As is so often the case with creative artists who are completely absorbed in their work, Vaughan Williams's outward life was not very remarkable during the last twenty years. If you had asked him about his day, he would have said that he got up at 6 a.m., or thereabouts, worked for an hour or so and then had breakfast. After reading the papers and skimming through the morning's post he would retire to his study and work until 12.30. After lunch he would take a walk, or work in the garden, or read quietly, or follow the example of his beloved cats and take a short nap. Then, after tea, he would work again until supper time.

There were no dramas. Every now and again he would shyly announce that a new work was nearing completion ('I have been foolish enough to write another symphony'), and then, because his handwriting was very untidy, copyists would be sent from London charged with the task of making a clean, readable score.

The first draft of a new Vaughan Williams work was always made in short-score (as well as full-score), so that it could easily be played on the piano, while he listened and tried to judge the effect as if he had never heard it before. Usually he would decide that there were weak spots ('dead wood') and that alterations would have to be made. He would return to work. Some weeks later a second performance would take place, this time before a select audience of friends whose judgement he trusted. They would naturally offer advice, or simply express enthusiasm. Sometimes he took notice of what they said, but, more often than not, he went his own way. He needed their presence as a kind of sounding-board against which he could test his own reactions. Once he had made up his mind, the revised orchestral full-score would soon be ready.

At this point the copyist's real work began: the preparation of a clean, neat score from which the work could be performed. Roy Douglas, one of Vaughan Williams's most trusted copyists, describes the problems:

He wrote his scores in ink and apparently very quickly, and many un-intentional discrepancies found their way on to the pages. Small things such as a missing bass clef after a tenor, arco missing after pizz, 'change to flute 2' missing after piccolo, clarinets in A mistransposed as in B flat, trumpet passages written on the horn's line for a few bars—all these were easily put right. At times, however, the complete woodwind or brass section or timpani would be playing up to the end of a right-hand page and over the page there would be blank bars; in these instances I would pencil in what I thought he might have intended as continuation and send it to him. Sometimes my guess was right, and sometimes entirely wrong. Again, perhaps one of those curious scale-passages would have a G sharp in the woodwind and a G natural in the strings, it was quite obvious that they ought to be the same. On consulting the piano score I might find that it had an F, or A, and not G at all: another query for the composer to answer. There were also occasions when I just could not read the notes. My favourite instance of this was in *Hodie*. I tried one unlikely-looking clarinet passage in B flat and in A, wondered if it had strayed from the cor-anglais line or the bassoon (in tenor or bass clef), but eventually had to give it up and ask him what the notes were meant to be. The reply came back 'Can't make this out at all, let's leave it out.' And we did.

Last Years

During rehearsals Vaughan Williams was quite prepared to make changes if he felt they were needed. Indeed, the more his hearing faded, the more anxious he became about such matters. But in the end the work would be to his satisfaction, and then its journey round the musical world could begin.

Two personal events stand out in the last years of his life. In 1951, Adeline, his wife, died at the age of eighty. She had suffered cruelly from ill-health during much of their married life. Devoted to her, he felt the loss deeply.

Fortunately there were friends to rally round, and one of them, the poet Ursula Wood, was especially close. She had enjoyed the warmth of Vaughan Williams's friendship when her own husband had died in 1942, and now it was her turn to offer comfort and sympathy. Eventually, in 1953, they married and settled down to a singularly happy life together.

Save for a triumphant tour of America, and several adventurous holidays, Vaughan Williams spent his last years in London. He sold 'The White Gates' and moved to a comfortable house in Hanover Terrace, Regent's Park. Leith Hill Place he had already handed over to the National Trust; and, typically, he had gone to immense trouble to set up a Trust of his own, so that his performing rights could be used to help music and musicians. He was now an old man—stooping slightly, his hair white and his face lined. When he died, on 20th August, 1958, he was well into his eighty-sixth year. Yet, such was the vigour of his personality and the solid assurance of his presence, it seemed to many as if music had suddenly lost one of its brightest and youngest spirits.

'Let us now praise famous men'

know - ledge. Such as found out mu-si-cal tunes, and re-

ci - ted ver-ses in wri - ting:_____ All these were hon-oured in their

gen - er - a - tions, and were the glo - - ry of their times._____

IX

The Man and His Music

When a composer is born at the beginning of a period of change and artistic revolution he faces peculiar difficulties, over and above the basic problem of learning how to express himself. He must find his own voice, but must do so against a background that may, at times, flatly contradict him. And when his composing career is as long as Vaughan Williams's was, the difficulties are multiplied time and again.

Consider the extraordinary length of his career and what it implies. When he was born, in 1872, Wagner had just completed the *Ring* cycle and was beginning the long struggle to create theatrical conditions fit to receive it. Of the leading symphonic composers, neither Tchaikovsky, Dvořák, nor Brahms had yet made any mature contribution to music—Brahms, indeed, was still four years distant from his first symphony. Moulded in the tradition of the great German classics, the musical world seemed, in 1872, settled and secure.

Between that date and the beginning of Vaughan Williams's own mature work, the language of music began the long series of stylistic convulsions that were to continue throughout his lifetime, and which still afflict us today. Romanticism, Impressionism, Expressionism, Neoclassicism; Tonality, Polytonality, Atonality: all offered themselves as solutions to the young composer. Before him lay, on the one hand, the persuasive delights of such revolutionary figures as Debussy, Bartók, Stravinsky, Schoenberg and Webern; and on the other, the reassuring traditionalism of Mahler, Elgar and Richard Strauss. To hack an individual path through this jungle of conflicting possibilities demanded an exceptionally cool head. Yet this is what Vaughan Williams did. He took what he needed, but remained undismayed by the conflict.

Consider, too, the extraordinary pattern of his career. His finest, most adventurous symphonies were written between the ages of sixty and seventy-five. Even if they live as long, most composers have by this age completed

64

Above left, Leith Hill Woods; *above right*, Vaughan Williams at the Three Choirs Festival; *below*, rehearsal of *The Lark Ascending* at the Three Choirs Festival, 1956

A rehearsal at Buffalo, U.S.A., in 1954

their best work; and many, like Sibelius, have retired from music altogether. Only Verdi shows a similar rising graph of achievement over the course of a long life.

And for sheer length of creative life, Vaughan Williams's example is probably unique. Eighty years lie between the music he left unfinished at his death and his first tentative steps as a boy of six. Moreover, they are eighty years of almost continuous exploration and development.

When a composer has been popular and successful in his lifetime, it usually happens that a reaction against his music sets in after his death. At its best, this reaction helps to right the balance of judgement. Less successful works can be seen clearly for what they are. The body of his real achievement is narrowed down to what is finest and most likely to endure. Sometimes, however, the reaction goes too far.

Ten years after his death, Vaughan Williams is less admired than he was, and to the point where some critics find it possible to overlook the enormous depth and range of his gifts.

To gain some idea of what he actually achieved, the listener should turn to the nine symphonies. Though, naturally enough, they share a great many common fingerprints, each explores a world of its own and offers a separate and unique experience. In his book on Vaughan Williams's music, Eric Blom goes so far as to compare them with Beethoven's for variety of mood and musical method. And exaggerated though the comparison may at first appear, it is, in fact, hard to contradict.

At the heart of Vaughan Williams's achievement and popularity is the sense that his music is always concerned with some urgent, necessary message. However tough his musical language—and the Fourth and Sixth symphonies are neither easy nor relaxing to listen to—there is the assurance that the difficulties are there because they are an intimate part of what has to be said. Thus he plays fair by his audience, and, as a result, the strength of his address is overwhelming.

It is hard, and possibly even unwise, to talk about a 'visionary' quality in a man's music. Either you feel it is there, and that the music has a specific message for you, or you do not. If you do not, then you may see in, for example, the *Pastoral Symphony* only what the composer Peter Warlock saw: 'a cow looking over a gate.' But if you do respond, then it will strike you that Warlock's judgement was singularly wide of the mark. That Vaughan Williams's music has this indefinable visionary quality seems to have been felt by too great a number of music-lovers to be dismissed as mere partisan fancy.

E

The Man and His Music

As a man, Vaughan Williams left an almost universally favourable impression. He was generous, warm-hearted, and passionate in his concern for music. Instances of his willingness to help young musicians abound, though he never advertised his generosity. In every sense, he graced the high position that public esteem placed him in.

He was, however, no plaster saint. He was quite capable of anger and indignation when something displeased him. A slipshod choir, or an inattentive orchestra, would soon bring down his wrath. He was capable, too, of remarks that were both barbed and witty—his confession that Delius's music always reminded him of 'a curate improvising' is an example, and far removed from the usual placid pictures of 'Uncle Ralph'.

For all its beauty and profundity, Vaughan Williams's music has a curious impersonal quality. The comparison with Elgar is instructive. Elgar looked inward at his own emotions, and drew his inspiration from them. Though never self-pitying, his music is always personal and in large measure autobiographical. He spoke in terms of his own 'stately sorrow'—a description that Vaughan Williams would never, in a thousand years, have applied to his own music.

On the contrary: Vaughan Williams looked outward and drew his inspiration from the world around him. Each of his symphonies is a comment on life as he saw it. His operas are concerned with other people's emotions—emotions that he could understand, but did not necessarily share. He did not even have to be personally involved in church dogma in order to write a great and convincing Mass. He is always the Pilgrim; journeying through life, observing it and drawing conclusions, but seldom, if ever, a slave to its delights and miseries.

It is probably this capacity for passionate detachment that enabled Vaughan Williams to develop an individual style at a time when the rest of the musical world was at sixes and sevens. And though it may have brought with it some limitations of feeling, it was to prove the source of his strength and the basis of his achievement.

Literary Postscript

During the course of a long professional life, Vaughan Williams often had reason to express his thoughts in words as well as music. He contributed articles to magazines, lectured and gave radio talks, wrote prefaces to other men's books, and even gathered together selections from his writings into books of his own. What he had to say is now of absorbing interest to anyone who wishes to study his character and his attitude to the art he loved. And one of the most revealing of all his writings is the essay on *Good Taste* which he contributed to *The Vocalist* in 1902. Who else would have spoken up like this:

> What is good taste? Is it a quality ever ascribed to a really great artist? Do we ever say of Beethoven or Mozart that their music is in good taste? And why is this? Because good taste is a purely artificial restriction which a composer imposes on himself when he imagines—rightly or wrongly— that his inspiration is not enough to guide him. A genius has no time to consider the claims of good taste; he is hurried blindly forward by the power of his own invention, and it is only when that fails he feels the absence of that prop on which the weak-kneed habitually stay themselves. What 'minor poet' among musicians would make such a fool of himself as to write the *Battle of Vittoria*? What well-brought-up composer but would blush for shame to have thought of anything so vulgar as some of Schubert's tunes? Yet how much would they not give to have invented one bar of *Erlkönig*, of the A Major Symphony?
>
> The truth is that the young Englishman is too musicianly. The 'musicianly' composer has studied the whole anatomy of inspiration, and has found out all the mechanical means by which beautiful music is produced. Equipped with this knowledge, he proceeds to build up compositions with yard-measure and plumb-line, quite forgetting that no man can make a living body out of dead clay unless he has first stolen some of the heavenly fire.

If a composer is naturally vulgar, let him be frank and write vulgar music instead of hedging himself about with an artificial barrier of good taste. If he is naturally trivial, let him not simulate a mock solemnity which is quite foreign to his nature. If every composer will be himself, his music will at all events be genuine. If it is of bad grain, no amount of veneer can alter its nature; if it is good oak it will not be improved by being made to look like mahogany.

Away, then, with good taste. Good taste is the heritage of critics, and a good critic is, proverbially, a bad composer. What we want in England is *real* music, even if it be only a music-hall song. Provided it possesses real feeling and real life, it will be worth all the off-scourings of the classics in the world.

R Vaughan Williams

From Hymn-tune Prelude: *Rhosymedre*

Suggestions for Further Reading

THE TWO most detailed and authoritative studies were published by Oxford University Press in 1964. They are:

R.V.W. A Biography of Ralph Vaughan Williams, by Ursula Vaughan Williams.

The Works of Ralph Vaughan Williams, by Michael Kennedy.

The most helpful short study of his life and works is published by J. M. Dent, in their *The Master Musicians Series* (1961): *Vaughan Williams*, by James Day.

The composer's collected writings are published by Oxford University Press in a paperback volume: *National Music*.

Heirs and Rebels (Letters written by Holst and Vaughan Williams), edited by Ursula Vaughan Williams and Imogen Holst and published by Oxford University Press (1959), though now out of print, is worth searching for in libraries and bookshops.

Summary of Vaughan Williams's Works

Dates are dates of composition

Symphonies

A Sea Symphony (1903–1909)
A London Symphony (1912–13; revised 1920 and 1933)
Pastoral Symphony (1922)
Symphony No 4, in F minor (1931–34)
Symphony No 5, in D (1938–43)
Symphony No 6, in E minor (1944–47)
Sinfonia Antartica (1949–52)
Symphony No 8, in D minor (1953–55)
Symphony No 9, in E minor (1956–57)

Solo Instruments and Orchestra

The Lark Ascending (Romance for Violin and Orchestra) (1914)
Violin Concerto in D minor (1924–25)
Flos Campi (Suite for Viola, Chorus, and small Orchestra) (1925)
Concerto for Piano and Orchestra (1926–31)
Concerto for Oboe and Strings (1944)
Romance for Harmonica, Strings and Piano (1952)
Concerto for Bass Tuba and Orchestra (1954)

Orchestral

Norfolk Rhapsody (1905–6)
The Wasps (Aristophanic Suite) (1909)
Fantasia on a theme of Thomas Tallis (1910; revised 1913 and 1919)
Job (A Masque for Dancing) (1927–30)
Five variants of 'Dives and Lazarus' (1939)
Partita for Double String Orchestra (1948)

Summary of Vaughan Williams's Works

Chorus and Orchestra

Toward the Unknown Region (1905–6)
Sancta Civitas (Oratorio) (1923–25)
Benedicite (1929)
Five Tudor Portraits (1935)
Dona Nobis Pacem (1936)
Serenade to Music (1938)
Hodie (1953–54)

Chamber Music

On Wenlock Edge (Tenor, piano and string quartet) (1909)
Phantasy Quintet (1912)
String Quartet in A minor (1942–44)
Sonata in A minor for Violin and Piano (1954)

Operas

Hugh the Drover (1910–14; revised up to 1956)
The Shepherds of the Delectable Mountains (1922)
Sir John in Love (1924–28)
Riders to the Sea (1925–32)
The Poisoned Kiss (1927–29; revised up to 1957)
The Pilgrim's Progress (completed 1949; revised 1952)

Index

Index